Thoughts written under Blacklight.

Syed amran Ali

BookLeaf Publishing

Presentation by *BookLeaf Publishing*

Web: www.bookleafpub.com

E-mail: info@bookleafpub.com

ISBN: 9789357212793

First edition 2023

DEDICATION

To my beautiful children Saffiyah & Adam

ACKNOWLEDGEMENT

For Bookleaf publishing for giving me to opportunity to have this created.
For my wife Michelle for always finding the right things for me at the right time.

PREFACE

A collection of thoughts over the years which were left on bits of paper and saved on different mobile phones over years. Jotted down in a form of poetry as a coping mechanism.

Coming back to some of my work after decades, I've grown fondly over them. These words have elevated over the years and have become precious over time

Having no academic training or education, I never considered my raw thinking could ever by published. it has been left on a dusty shelf... Until now.

7-3 = fourth

Seven days does not exist, for the world exists in three days,
We live with a time-traveling mentality and remember in three ways.

The past: a place that exists in memory, a place that holds reflection,
where we relive ourselves, appreciate what happened, and are the creator of affection.

It's a place where pain has now expired, but not forgotten, forming a safe space,
reliving the footprints of yesterday without leaving a new trace.

We take photos, to capture the present, in a bid to capture time,
we do so so that we can still remember, days once upon a time.

The present: The here and right now, where we take steps towards diamonds or dust,
working on ourselves before destiny is revealed, a place where we constantly adjust.

Our footsteps are seeding the choices we choose
every step we take,
we hope the seeds affect a positive future, in the
hope our present doesn't break.

We plan for the future, and even though we can
never see it, we constantly live In the now.
The past becomes regret, and tomorrow becomes
a threat, ruining our present somehow.

The future: the final day, a day we never seem to
step in,
it is unmade, It has no space or sound, a place
free from sin.

We have a chance to rectify our thoughts,
understand the consequences of future actions,
with foresight, we can foresee a present action,
so that we receive a fruitful reaction.

In a bid to reduce the everyday sin we create, we
are a catastrophic producer,
we do so, to appreciate the present, and to be
grateful we don't make such a future.

We live in three days, and now you see the facts
of human life, time is really short for us,
there's no time for being angry, no time for being
negative, no time to have drama or fuss.

So remember this life and take pictures, live
your life like a present, and plant wonderful
seeds to nourish the upcoming,
because one day, we will pass from the third day
into a new fourth, the final day of becoming.

.

I will always wait.

My vessel has expired, my body maybe gone,
I've only been released to where I truly belong.

We are all made up of star dust, including you
and I.
I can finally travel to that nebula,
the great cats eye.

Now every night you can look up and I will be
there sparkling in the sky.
It is why you shouldn't cry, because this was
never a goodbye.

Our vessels will expire, our essence is returned,
I'm just ahead today.
So I'm waiting here, until you arrive so that we
can start to play.

Breathing back control.

Bring down your entire senses with each passing breath,
notice that stillness along side your life, as though your close to death.

Hold on to that stillness, centre in your soul,
remove ego away from yourself, so that you can take back control.

Your soul is constricted, like rivers with multiple dams,
spend time in silence and override those auto programmes.

Set aside your burdens, and all your formalities,
give yourself a break from your multiple personalities.

Your body has driven on autopilot like a captain to her vessel,
Its wandering around the universe alone, without a guide for it to nestle.

It's not meant to lead the way, your mind has
long rested,
It needs to unlearn everything the body has
manifested.

So breath deep, inhale, and check in with your
soul,
Allow your body to reunite with your mind, and
make yourself whole.

Dig Deeper

Happiness is sought, by seeking something very stable,
so we search for stability in anything which will enable,
A trigger to our happiness, a feeling we must hold,
like a warm bright fire, keeping us away from the cold.

But this fire keeps flickering, burning high then low,
how do I steady this warm fiery glow?

Should I fuel it by a career, will happiness reside there?
Being told what to do, what to have, and even what to wear?

Will I find that light from a companion instead?
Having to compromise how much light I should see ahead?

They say financial stability is everything,
because absolutes are made from money,
but no amount of money in the world can change
rainy days into sunny.

We externalise everything we do, our happiness
is dependent on validations,
we look over the shoulders of others and make
contrasting observations.

You have to dig deeper, so that you can come to
realise,
that happiness is found as you breathe and
internalise.

You can light you own fire, and protect it from
any gust,
you can control your own path, and when to
adapt and adjust.

Try to not depend on anyone, to prop up your
smile.
Because the day they go, happiness is taken
away with them for awhile.

Dig deep, and start planting your own seeds,
Create strong roots so that you can meet your
own needs.

Things can go wrong, even with the best laid plans.
If security is everything, why leave it in someone else's hands?

Create roots which are strong, thick, and full of ability,
so that nothing and nobody can hold the power to uproot your internal stability.

Leaning inwards

Bathed in beautiful scenery,
A place my mind wants to be.

Expanding the reach of my heart,
To places, far apart.

In a world that can be very mean,
I've stopped looking to others to lean.

I've noticed nobody else would,
care as much as I can ever could.

The more my mind learns and knows,
the more my universe inside grows.

I've started to fall in love with the world again,
because I've started to love my world within.

Finding myself again is a blissful prize,
I can once again view it with grateful eyes.

Anxiety

My brain is soaked with anxiety,
flooding my every senses in its entirety.

Telling my body that I need to do something right,
Keeping me awake so that I'm very productive at night.

They stop me from procrastinating by overloading my perceptions with fears,
they tell me to get this task done so that the fog in my heart clears.

A sludge like entity masquerading as motivation in disguise,
telling me to run in all directions, even though I'm completely immobilised.

...My anxiety has taken over...

I need to make a call...1.2.3.4,
I calmly breathe, as I walk down my emotional corridor.

Many pathways to choose, with differently
elevated floors,
I need to find the control centre for all these
open doors.

Ive finally found him... were talking and
connecting...
My spiritual companion whispered,
"its okay lets start correcting".

He whispers into my mind, sending me nostalgic
and soothing views,
transcending my mind, back into time, exploring
memories to reuse.

Time travels differently here, starting from a
middle of a moment,
A chance to rewrite stories, to relive moments in
need of atonement.

It is time to step away from here, to be outside
of my mind,
so that I can make use of my new thoughts of
being self compassionate and kind.

My Anxiety is dried up for the day, I'm looking
forward to tomorrow...

Cigars & Stars

Vapours dance in the starry sky as I smoke my cigar,
finding myself lost up there pondering who we are.

The stirring of my thoughts, are inspired by the stillness of the galaxy,
contemplation compliments my mind, as I build a universe to memory.

The mind is the only instrument which doesn't dull with every use,
Its a fascinating concept that a mind sharpens from wear, tear and abuse.

Sharpened like a sword or like the tail of a comet,
my mind is shifting out of balance pulling me away from whats logic.

I think further than whats rational, I think further than reason,
I think of gods perfect design and the miracles of each season.

The two opposing forces take refuge in my
mind.
one to correct with reason, and the other to
believe in gods design.

But colliding these forces together, I have
smashed the impurities in my head,
transcending my realisation, by separating the
rational and the actual instead.

I have become a complete mind yet its still
unbelievably empty.
So I still hold unto my cigar, in hopes to ponder
aplenty.

If todays thoughts are these, I cant wait for
tomorrows cigar session,
if the stars visit me again like this night,
then new knowledge will be in my possession.

Centred?

Am I balanced, or am I a contradiction?
Because I accept both sides of many situations.

I see both sides of the same coin, flickering in the air,
spinning as one and not a separate pair.

Too much good isn't good for you one should know,
that's why evil is created, to appreciate the time you know.

This cat and mouse game we've been playing for years,
chasing for the truth, or running from our fears.

We MOUSE, we avoid, we dodge confrontation,
with no new information we can continue without hesitation.

when death visits us, you can put your hands up and say "I never knew it"
you carried no burden of knowledge, evading every bullet.

Visit the other side of yourself, don't avoid and deflect,
you can at least show your worth, instead of running in neglect.

We CAT, we chase and force others our right,
we speak out possible truths, with conviction, power and might.

We become an enigmatic ego, a powerful pride,
we walk over the innocent and powerless with every stride.

We forget the truth as we fall in love with our power,
we plunder lies and dig away at delicate flowers.

A contradiction is essential and vital,
otherwise we would never learn what's really inciteful.

Blasphemy, ethically, morally neutered,
stuck in our ways, and stopping us from being tutored.

Call me balanced, grounded, or indecisive, there all rolled into one,
I'm not someone you can simply categorise and place a finger on.

My layers create a problem for you, but it's a blessing for me you see,
at least I'm never the same person, even my reflection is new to me.

Auto & me

To empower yourself is to power the mind,
by removing yourself away from this current
design.

My character has been on autopilot recently,
making itself up to appear more able,
It was admirable what my body was trying to do,
but all it did was play a label.

Flying a person even I wasn't aware of, I was
just happy to go along,
the flight was comfortable, it was harmonious, it
flew a sweet song.

But something was wrong, I felt someone in
front of me,
but it wasn't possible, for I'm in control, I control
these eyes I see.

In actuality auto was still in control, my mind
was strapped in the seat,
I didn't want to lose this feeling, this happiness
in every heartbeat.

The flight felt some turbulence, as auto studied
it's waves,
but wait.. I know what these turbulences are, I
know how this current behaves.

My eyes flutter as auto struggles to manoeuvre
in this flight plan,
why can I not pass them so easily as I know I
can?

Strapped in the seat, flicking off the autopilot
switch,
my flight tumbles, as I realise that auto has made
my character glitch.

Switched to manual, my blurry eyes try to steer
the wheel,
my eyes are adjusting to the pains my heart
didn't feel.

The flight flies amongst fire, lightning erupting
everywhere,
where have I been all this time, gasping as I
stare.

Time to steer away from this hellish mess,
time to take control of myself, to change what I
have come to detest.

I will become myself again soon, as I fly away
from these scars,
I will see my myself fly away, and cruise
amongst the stars. x x

Mind Ownership

The great thing about being single my mind is
only mine to bare,
when attached to someone, you have to really
compromise and share.

Your thoughts are truly not your own, chaining
your potential for another,
you think for two, you act for two, you have
another person to consider.

Your power to yourself decreases as the other
one takes over you,
the chamber that once held your dreams, now
the other one invades you too.

"Be true to yourself", a simple task, which is not
available anymore,
being 'yourself' would be just you, but your not
alone anymore.

Being yourself is history, for now there is a role
you must play,
so fetch on that mask to hide yourself, and
become the new display.

For honesty does not win hearts your only
reward is the untruth,
the mask you chosen to hide behind encourages
and reveals the truth.

We all play the nice game, to win the hearts of
our mark,
your not the only who knows that lies create the
love spark.

We build the foundation on a lie, and then cover
it up with a blanket of love,
then someone gets hurt unravelling the cover.
Revealing the foundation was not so tough.

I will wait until someone finds me, someone
who wants a whole figure,
not compromised as a half, but someone who
can appreciate my true vigor.

People rather be two half people, so they
become one whole,
but I would rather be two full people, exploring
each others soul.

If you cut away half of the earth, how many
wonders of the world would you miss?
so please let me keep myself, as you will earn
the recipe of true bliss.

Cats

To know life, you need to know what it's like to connect to this vibrant earth,
to be linked to to another life outside of yours, a different time to your birth.

To connect with man, it's one thing. A simple communication is enough,
but to connect with a beast is vastly another, it can be challenging and tough.

Kitty was one such feline, moody, tough but loyal,
her name came from within her soul, she was born to be a royal.

She was in my life at the time before I was someone people knew,
phasing and transitioning into who I am now,
she's the only one who's seen me through.

Do you really know who I was then? my words are your only guide,
she was always there watching me,
she knew things I could never hide.

She wasnt moved by money or even gifts,
though maybe one treat or ten.
Her life was full of meanings and words, which could easily dry out a pen.

She stored beautiful memories as cameras could not,
she exuded life and feeling that could not be bought.

Even though she may have looked at you like she's hatching a plot,
you knew she was always there for you, laying on every sun spot.

Kitty was everything. So she was given everything. The day she was lost so was I,
nothing is the opposite of everything and that's how I felt inside.

But she was my everything, all the memories we made, completing a timeline,
I'm so grateful to have set moments in life which was just hers and mine.

School girl.

My baby girl has grown into a small
little girl,
the clam that I once was is getting too
small for my pearl.

Shes reaching out, she is full of
imagination,
She doesn't want to follow my direction
or destination.

Shes only three how is it already time,
she has dreams that are already
outside of mine,

day dreaming of scooters and skates,
climbing our next doors neighbors
gates.

Angry tantrums for not having her way,
articulate descriptions of whatever
she has to say.

She's become a smart kid, so lets see
what pre school has to offer,
I hope they bring out the world in her,
for my beautiful pearl to discover.

The Son in a spacesuit

A soul has been forged, fashioned into a playful boy,
we always ponder and wonder whenever he plays with a toy.

But a toy to him can be sponge or a measuring tape,
he provides a beautiful relief, a joyful secret escape.

His new toddler legs, as if he is always on a hike,
he even says yeah to the things he doesnt even like.

Giving you the thumbs up but really sideways,
and staring at you with his expressionionless botox gaze.

when he stumbles, you will know about it though,
even if he falls on his head, he will point at his elbow.

Holding his star pillow before every nap,
prepping his rocket to dreamland all seated and strapped.

When Adam dreams, I hope he is dreaming of rocket ships and stars,
as much as the happiness he gets from touching a random persons car.

I hope his blanket he snuggles reminds him of planets and space,
so that his feet lands on our hearts each night,
and leaves us with a trace.

THE RED OCEAN SEA DIVER

I WISH YOU COULD SEE, THE FANTASTIC
VIEW OF MY SEA,
I WISH IT WAS AS UNDERSTANDABLE TO
YOU, AS IT IS TO ME.

THIS OXYGEN-RICH SEA THAT I DIVE,
PROVIDES ME THE AIR AND WILL TO
SURVIVE.

I HAVE BECOME MORE THEN YOU
COULD EVER REALISE,
EVEN THE MIRROR DOESN'T REFLECT
ME FOR IT CANNOT RECOGNISE.

I CAN SEE MY OWN ICEBERG HERE
DOWN BELOW,
MORE THAN JUST SCRATCHING THE
SUPERFICIAL SNOW.

MY PERSONALITY SHINES IN THAT RED
MIST,
AN ADVENTURE THAT I WILL NEVER
RESIST.

I AM A PIRATE LONGING TO ESCAPE TO
THE SEA,
IT IS AN ADDICTION AND WHOLE FULLY
BEAUTIFUL TO ME.

A SEA VOYAGER, POINTING MY SWORD
TOWARDS THE OCEAN,
A DECLARATION OF UTTER DEVOTION.

THE RELEASE THAT I GET IS BETTER
THAN ANY DRUG I CAN EVER CRAVE,
IT RELIEVES THE REJECTION I FEEL
WHEN MY BODY MISBEHAVES.

I LONG TO CUT DEEP AND WATCH MY
SKIN SPLIT INTO TWO,
I AM THE CAPTAIN OF MY VESSELS AND
MY VEINS TOO.

The Old Classic

My heart tank is running low, its been running
its course,
travelling on empty, fueled with only remorse.

The tracks are started to slow,
and now the engine is ready to blow.

what do I do now, I thought I had a lot of love to
give,
the mileage has started to show, now my engine
is about to give.

what do you do when you are an old timer like
me,
with nobody to love your back log or history.

Ive been a owner of many, and now its started to
show,
will I ever be loved like the first time I was put
on show.

Im a classic and I want to be handled with care,
but I know, im also old, as to which nobody will
care.

what will become of me, what can I do,
Im not in a position where I can pull through.

I know someone out there is searching for a vintage like me,
I hope to be found soon, where they can showcase me.

Be proud of an old timer who is set in his ways,
to be loved for the classic styles, where once I had my ways.

Now I will show you how love was meant to be,
because its lost in todays times, are you glad you have found me?

Meditation Train

We need to let go of these daily strains,
we are ending up home exhausted with daily
sprains.

Instead of taking pills to escape your migraine,
imagine yourself on a beautiful night train.

Guided through the stars on it's rail way lanes,
travelling to exotic places from Bahrain to
Spain.

Take this moment as a chance to refrain,
from worries, negatively and other pains.

Every choice you make has two set lanes,
A decision you must take before you detrain.

You can look at your day with dislike & distain,
or be grateful to what you've already obtained.

Look for the goodness, even in within the rain,
thank you for choosing the midnight mediation
train.

With Timing

It is your perception, who are the owners of
time,
you can control how much you want, and how
much you want to rewind.

Nothing can move time forward until you are
truly ready,
time wont runs past you even if your thoughts
race unsteady.

Stay focused, so you can place time firmly
beneath your feet,
don't wallow in your past, and leave time in a
loop or in repeat.

Ask yourself, who am I currently.. Where am I
now,
this will slow down time, to keep you in the here
and now.

Move on, or stay put, it's truly your choice,
staying doesn't hurt you, Just listen to your own
voice.

They tell you to get on with life. But they don't know how you feel,
sometimes living In the past is the only place that's real.

It's predictable, it's safe, because you can't develop new pain,
and one of the reasons why we always remain the same.

Time has no power if you do not accept it, it has to wait for you,
don't let you mates push you in a rush, as time isn't rushing you.

Your life is ticking away, so keep your eye on the clock,
soon, with time and thought, the real you will be unlocked.

So don't pursue what's unnecessary to you, and waste your time in misery,
in this brief moment your life is in, become a memorable legacy.

Our clouds

You realise how much life goes by,
when you look up at the sky.

Watching the clouds play in the blue,
teasing the sun and blocking it's view.

Feeling the breeze blow the clouds along,
as the clouds dance and swerves to its windy
song.

When it's time to sing, they can play a ballad as
loud as thunder,
an electrical emotion displayed in a grey
coloured wonder.

They too have the need to burst into tears,
missing us as they move on, sending us farewell
cheers.

We look up as they look down, as life passes us
by,
they sing and dance, and also share a teary
goodbye.

Soul, Heart, and Shield

My body is on fire, my heart is ready to declare,
the broken pieces are in a sad state of affair.

I've damaged my soul through all the wear & tear,
as my heart constructs a beautiful dream into a nightmare.

Having nobody to love anymore, the heart has fixed it's gaze inside,
looking for something to consume, to create an apartiad.

It starts to love the soul, but in a very toxic way,
feeding itself warmth, and reducing the soul into decay.

The heart sells the soul lies, my soul smiles, my heart sighs,
the soul answers to it's call and readily commits to it all.

But as always they argue and conflicts arise,
bickering so much that they just reject and despise.

My soul and my heart are having a toxic affair,
It's darkened my soul, broken beyond repair.

A chemical seeps into the body, paralysing the heart and soul,
the 'I don't give a damn' nuke has started to role.

An obliterating force which closes my eyes,
forcing me to be less aware,
as it separates the conflict in me, the less and less I care.

It pistons my strength, easing my despair,
charging my body and everything in the air.

A mushroom cloud is formed as it destroys the bad and the good,
this depressive numbness makes me less and less understood.

Resentment is a lonely system to use,
pushing everyone away, as I shout and abuse.

But the heart finally, finds a mark,
sensing the pulse of another like a ferocious shark.

Turning them into my heart shield, so that it
cannot eat me alive,
the soul can be left alone now, to discover and to
thrive.

But im indestructible now for I hold a heart
shield,
someone who protects my ego when im out on
the battlefield.

I hold a secret power card, a warm safety net,
so I can be myself, I see no fear or perceive a
threat.

My calm soul and my aggressive heart has
stopped its row,
as my shield blocks its endless war, giving my
peace for now.

She forms a fortified shield, protecting all who
attack my heart,
my little savour, my soul healer, a place for my
life to start.

Lost in Thought

We are all so unhappy because we know too much,
we are lost in our maturity, growing more out of touch.

Im constructing a wall by all the intelligence I collect,
It blocks the sounds and sights of fun, as I ponder and reflect.

Im creating many pathways to defy the single road we all go through,
creating multiple and complicated twists and turns, the more facts I knew.

We encourage others to mature, so that we can relate with them,
condemning the ignorant for having fun, even though were knowingly envied them.

We are winning, bringing them into world away from mystery,
making them mature, because we enjoy the company of misery.

The judgement of others have made me this way,
I was impressing all my back biters,
I've learned allot, to which I cannot unlearn,
making me a skeptical writer.

Tis why we have children I'd wager, to see
happiness welcome us again,
I wish I never bothered to grow up, as I watch
them grin without any pain.

It's painful to think so much, that my life isn't
spent playfully,
to always see consequences, As I watch others
engage pointlessly.

I must take a leaf out an ignorants page, I need
to learn something,
that there is no beauty in sadness, no growth in
fear, no honour in suffering.

Heavenly Daughters

They see the blessing you gave to them
As they hold each others hand,
They smile and cherish your priceless gift, if
only you could understand.

They love you, cherish you, and appreciate their
new home, more than a millions years of life,
without birth, heaven could not exist,
you have given them peace, away from earths
strife.

There's nothing more precious then the gift of
heaven, and you have done that twice,
so shed those tears in pride and not sorrow, your
have guaranteed heaven with your sacrifice.

Many have children, and many grow old, but
many do not pass the angels gate,
you have been blessed by giving them the best,
and the only possible fate.

They have your blood, flowing through their
veins, but have no recollection of the earth,
the best of two things provided for them
They don't understand pain, only love since
birth.

Love is the only magic that connects us to
heaven, your daughters, live that love,
don't feel sad for them, be proud, as they dance
and play up above.

You breathed life into them, you carried them
and raised them, in such a small time,
they now look from the inside of the windows of
heaven, watching over you from time to time.

One second of heaven can only be compared to a
thousand earth years,
the moment they blink, a thousand years will
pass, as you arrive, they will wipe away your
tears.

They will say "welcome home father" and listen
to how much you missed them,
centuries will walk as you sit and talk, showing
your love as you kiss them.

They will say "I missed you mother" as they
watch her tears drop like rain,
she will hug them, and squeeze them, vowing to
never let them go again.

We are a family again, we can create a new
memory lane, a scenery without any pain,
now all your waiting for is a simple blink, and
you will all be together again.

www.ingramcontent.com/pod-product-compliance
Lightning Source LLC
Chambersburg PA
CBHW051741130826
49812CB00033B/951
9789357212793